This book is for Timothy and Scott.

All inquiries should be addressed to:
Barron's Educational Series, Inc.
250 Wireless Boulevard
Hauppauge, New York 11788

Library of Congress Catalog Card No. 92-8603

International Standard Book No. 0-8120-6215-9

Library of Congress Cataloging-in-Publication Data
Elias, Joyce.
    Whose toes are those? / Joyce Elias : illustrated by Cathy
Sturm.
        p.   cm.
    Summary: Pictures of the toes of various animals are
accompanied by poems that describe but do not name the
animal. On the following page the animal is named and fully
revealed in its natural habitat.
    ISBN 0-8120-6215-9
    1. Animals—Juvenile poetry. 2. Children's poetry, American.
[1. Animals—Poetry. 2. American poetry.] I. Sturm, Cathy, ill.
II. Title.
PS3555.L43W48   1992
811'.54—dc20   92-8603
                                                          CIP
                                                          AC

PRINTED IN HONG KONG
2345 9927 98765432

Whose Toes Are Those?

Joyce Elias
Illustrated by Cathy Sturm

BARRON'S

His giant jaw snaps
While he sits near the swamps
He takes long naps
Then slithers and romps.

His thick and rough skin
Is scaly and green
He has a thin tail
And sometimes he's mean.

His snout makes a snort
And his body is long
He has four short legs
And his claws are strong.

Whose toes are those?

Alligator

He has arms that
Are really wings
His beady eyes
Scare all kinds of things.

He mostly likes
To come out at night
Vampires love him
He's such a fright!

Upside down
He hangs around
Those paws
Are claws!

Whose toes are those?

Bat

"SMACK"

He is so big
And oh so gray
Most of all
He loves to play.

Peanuts are
What he likes to eat.
Do you see
His great big feet?

Whose toes are those?

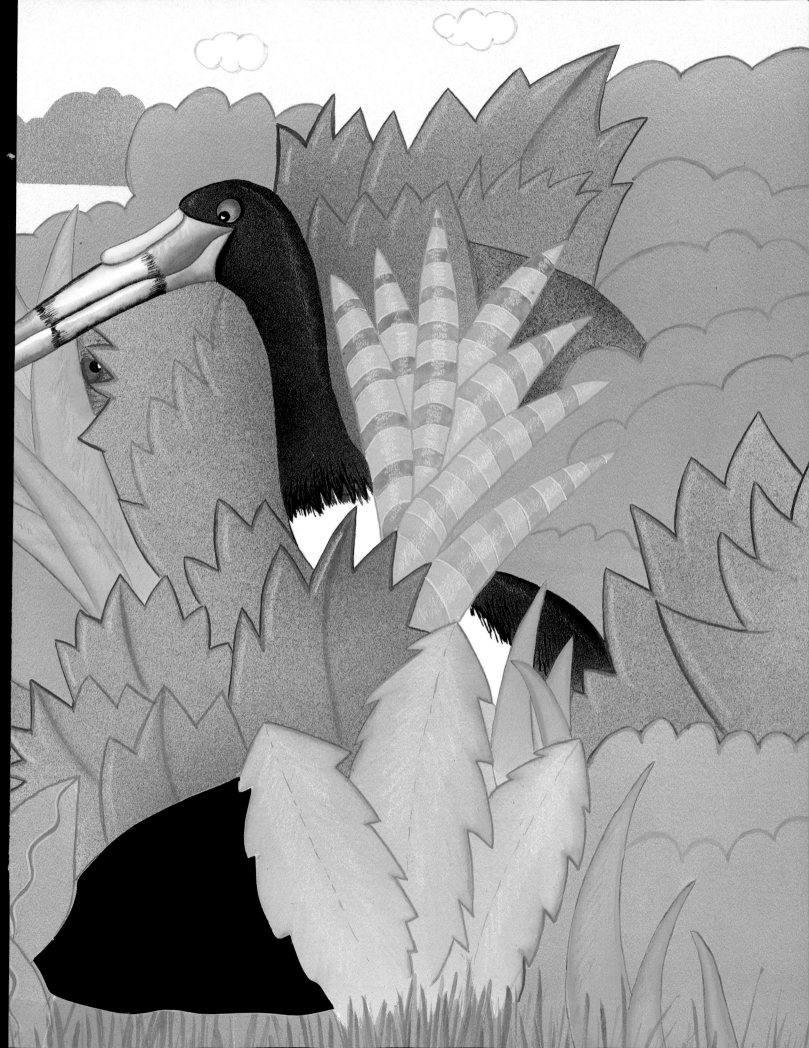

Elephant

He lives near a pond
Where it's damp and wet
His color is green
As green can get.

His long, long tongue
Catches tons of flies
He sees everything
With big bulging eyes.

Hippity hippity hippity hop
His four webbed feet
Help him flip and flop.

Whose toes are those?

Frog

She looks kind of like
A giant mouse
Though she would not
Live in a house.

She carries her baby
In a great big pocket
She springs off the ground
Just like a rocket!

Whose toes are those?

Kangaroo

In the jungle
He is the king
He roars much louder
Than any old thing.

His golden mane
Glows in the sun
On the chase
He can really run!

Whose toes are those?

Lion

He's almost human
And very spunky
When he walks
His walk is funky.
His feet are his hands
That's how he stands.

Whose toes are those?

Monkey

She's black and white
And furry and round
Her paws are padded
They don't make a sound.

Bamboo forests
Are where she rests
Bamboo snacks
Are what she likes best!

Whose toes are those?

Panda

It looks like he's wearing
A black tux with tails
He waddles on land
And can swim with the whales.

He has two little wings
On each of his sides
When he swims in the water
He paddles and glides.

He eats lots of fish
With his pointy beak
And uses it too
When he wishes to speak.

His big yellow feet
Are webbed, wide and flat.
Whose toes would go
With feet like that?

Penguin

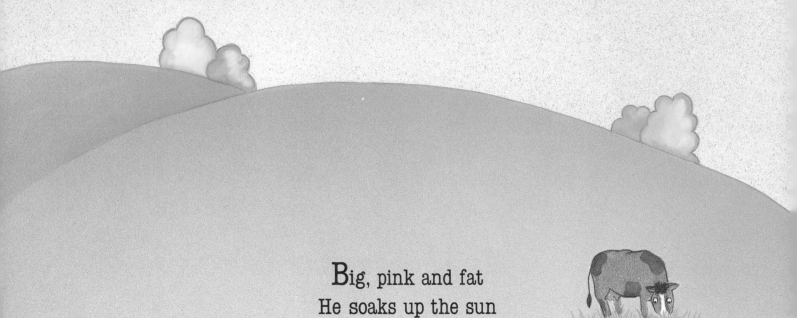

Big, pink and fat
He soaks up the sun
Rolling in mud
Is lots of fun.

He snorts and sighs
With his pushed in snout
And once in a while
He'll run all about.

His pen is always
Such a big mess
Whose toes are those?
Please take a guess.

Pig

In a dark corner
Where it's quite dry
She builds a large web
To catch a fly.

Her eight legs creep
Her eight legs crawl
Up a tall tree
Up a tall wall.

Looking for more
Small bugs to eat
She moves around
On tiny feet.

Whose toes are those?

Spider